Python Academy

Learning The Basics Of Python

Programming

Table Of Contents

Introduction

I want to thank you and congratulate you for downloading the book, *"Learn the Basics of Python Programming in 2 Weeks"*.

This book contains proven steps and strategies on how to write and run programs in Python. There are sample codes and programs that you can use as guidelines.

This book also contains an introduction to the programming language, including a brief history and the fundamentals of Python. It also contains detailed explanations about the features found in Python.

Thanks again for downloading this book, I hope you enjoy it!

Chapter 1: Introduction to Python

If you are looking for a general purpose, high level programming language with code readability as its main focal point, you should consider Python. It has a syntax that allows you to express concepts using fewer lines of code than other programming languages, such as C, C++, and Java. It supports a wide range of programming paradigms, thereby encompassing imperative, functional and object-oriented programming. Also, it features a comprehensive standard library, a dynamic tape system and an automatic memory management.

There are plenty of interpreters you can use for installation on different operating systems; hence, it is possible for you to execute Python on various systems. You can even make use of third-party applications. If you do not want to install an interpreter, you can package the code into standalone executable programs so that you can effectively distribute Python-based software to different environments.

A Brief History of the Python Programming Language

Python was developed by Guido van Rossum in the late 1980's. It was initially just a Christmas project. Van Rossum wanted an interpreter for a scripting language that C and UNIX hackers will use. His little project eventually upgraded to Python 2.0, which was released on October 2000. This new version had a complete garbage collector and Unicode support. Python 3.0, also called Python 3000 and py3k, was released in December 2008 and had features that were backported to versions 2.6 and 2.7.

Why should you Use Python?

Programming languages exist for a reason. Python, for instance, was developed to allow programmers to create efficient and productive codes. Its main objective is to help beginners learn a programming language easily and quickly. Due to this less learning time, you can create more useful applications that will be difficult to do with more obscure and complicated programming languages.

With Python, you can also benefit from less development time when coding applications. As mentioned earlier, Python has fewer lines of code than C, C++, and Java. Its codes are actually five to ten times shorter; thus, making it more efficient and less complicated. You get to spend less time in developing applications and more time tweaking and improving them.

When it comes to checking for bugs and errors, it is crucial for the programming language that you use to be easy to read and comprehend. If the programming language is too complicated, you may have a hard time coding and checking your program. With Python, codes are much easier to read and write; hence, you can easily interpret the codes and make the necessary changes.

Furthermore, Python has many other uses. It is ideal for scripting applications that are browser-based, creating great user interfaces and rough application examples, interacting with databases, working with XML and designing mathematic, engineering and scientific applications.

Python vs. C#, Java, and Perl

You may find comparing programming languages with one another to be a subjective task. Usually, their differences are a matter of personal preference. Nonetheless, there are times when such comparisons are backed up by scientific data. Anyway, you have to keep in mind that an all-encompassing programming language does not exist. As a programmer, you just have to find one that works best for your goals or needs.

C#

If you have a background in Java, you may notice that C# and Java are highly similar. Then again, C# still has its own advantages and disadvantages compared to Java. Microsoft claims that their primary objective in developing C# is to produce a better version of C and C++. Compared to C#, however, Python has better scientific and engineering applications and better multiplatform support. It is more extendable when it comes to using C, C++ and Java. It is easier to learn and comprehend, and it allows the use of various computer environments. It also has more concise codes.

Java

Programmers consider Java as a one-stop shop programming language. For many years, they have searched for something that can be run and written anywhere and they found Java, which can perform well in different platforms and computer environments. With this being said, Python is also a one-stop shop programming language. It is very similar to Java, except that it has more concise codes and it is easier to learn and comprehend. It is much faster to develop and it has improved data boxes or variables that can store different data types that are useful when running applications.

PERL

PERL stands for Practical Extraction and Report Language. It is a programming language that is suitable for acquiring and processing data from another database. In comparison, Python is better than PERL because it is easier to read, implement, learn and understand. It has better Java integration and data protection. It also has less platform-specific biases.

Why Python is Ideal for Beginners?

If you have just started programming, you may want to consider Python. It is ideal for beginners because it has a consistent and simple syntax and vast standard library that allows you to do multiple projects. The assignments involved are not limited to the usual four-function calculator and check balancing programs.

As you get used to writing programs in Python, you will realize that it is actually easy to make realistic applications. The interactive interpreter will also allow you to test language features. In Python, you can concentrate on essential programming skills, such as programming decomposition and data type design, and fundamental concepts, including procedures and loops.

Since Python involves the use of multiple libraries and system calls, you can develop applications with interfaces that are easy to program. You can also complete tasks necessary for the application programming interface (API).

Do not worry if you have never used any other programming language before. Even people with no prior programming knowledge or experience can easily grasp the fundamentals of the Python programming language.

As for the installation, Python is easy to install. Most UNIX and Linux distributions actually include it in their package. If you purchase a Windows computer from Hewlett-Packard (HP), you can readily use Python as it comes pre-installed with the system.

To make things easier for you, you should study how to use the text editors as well as the integrated development environments (IDEs). It will also be helpful to read programming books with sample codes and programs.

Regarding copyright, the developers of Python allow programmers to do whatever they want with the source, as long as they do not forget to include the copyrights. The copyright rules are not that strict. You can even sell copies in binary and source form, as well as products involving Python use. However, if you wish to use the logo, see to it that you obtain permission.

Python is highly stable. In fact, it is stable enough for regular use. You can expect a new version within six to eighteen months. The developers issue bug fix releases to ensure that the newer versions are better than the previous ones.

If you want to perform a static analysis or search for bugs, you can use Pylint or

PyChecker. The previous is a tool that checks the module to see if it abides by the coding standard as well as allow the customization of plug-ins. The latter is a static analysis tool that finds bugs in the source code.

So now that you have learned about the fundamentals of the programming language, you may still wonder how Python got its name. Was Guido van Rossum fond of pythons? Well, he was actually fond of the television show called Monty Python's Flying Circus, not the reptile.

During the time of Python's development, he was reading scripts from the comedy series and thought that 'Python' will be a suitable name since it was short, unique and has the right amount of mystery. In fact, references to the comedy show are allowed and actually encouraged in documentations.

Chapter 2: Syntax

Python has a simple and straightforward syntax. It even encourages programmers to write programs without using prepared or boilerplate codes. The print directive is actually the simplest of all directives. It prints out lines and includes newlines. You may notice that the print directive is different in the new major versions of the programming language.

Python 2.0 is the more common version while Python 3.0 supports the latest features and is more semantically correct. Anyway, the print statement is not considered as a function in version 2.0; hence, you can invoke it without including parentheses in your code. On the other hand, the print statement is considered as a function in version 3.0; hence, you have to use parentheses if you wish to invoke it.

Interactive Mode Programming

You can execute your programs in different modes. If you invoke the interpreter without passing the script file as a parameter, this is what you will get:

```
$ python
Python 2.4.3 ( #1, Nov 11 2010, 13:34:43 )
[GCC 4.1.2 20080704 ( Red Hat 4.1.2 – 48 )]
on linux2
Type "help", "copyright", "credits" or
"license" for more information.
>>>
```

When you see this prompt, you can type in your desired text then press Enter. In this example, we will be using the words 'Monty Python and the Holy Grail'.

```
>>> print "Monty Python and the Holy Grail" ;
```

Take note that if you are using a newer version of the programming language, you need to use opening and closing parentheses with your print statement, such as in the following:

```
>> print ( "Monty Python and the Holy Grail" ) ;
```

Regardless of which version you are using, if you run the sample code shown above, you will get the following output:

Monty Python and the Holy Grail

Script Mode Programming

If you invoke the interpreter with a script parameter, the script will start to execute and continue to run until it is done. When it is done, the interpreter will not be active anymore. Consider the following example. The sample program is written in a script and has a *.py* extension:

print "Monty Python's Flying Circus";

If you type in the above given source code in a test.py file and run it as

$ python test. Py

you will obtain the following output:

Monty Python's Flying Circus

Another way to execute scripts is to modify
the *.py* file, such as:

#! /usr /bin /python

print "Monty Python's Flying Circus";

If you run it as

$ chmod + x test.py
$ ./test.py

you get the following output:

Monty Python's Flying Circus

Identifiers

An identifier is basically used to determine functions, variables, modules, classes, and any other objects. It begins with an underscore (_) or a letter. It is then followed by digits, underscores, zero or other letters. As a programmer, feel free to use any letter or digit. You can use uppercase and lowercase letters.

However, you cannot use punctuations and special characters, such as @, $, and %, within the identifiers. In addition, Python is a case sensitive programming language. This means that you have to be careful when you use uppercase and lowercase letters in your codes. For instance, *wendy*, *Wendy*, and *WENDY* are all the same name and yet they are regarded as three different identifiers in Python.

Rules for Identifiers in Python

There are several rules that you have to abide by when writing programs in Python:

- The class name must always start with an uppercase character while the rest of the identifiers must start with a lowercase character.

- The identifier is private if it starts with just one leading underscore.

- The identifier is strongly private if it starts with two leading underscores.

- The identifier is a language-defined special name if it ends with two trailing underscores.

Reserved Words

Take note that there are certain words you cannot use as constants, identifier names, or variables in Python. All keywords are also written using lowercase letters. The following is a table of the reserved words in the programming language:

And	Assert	Break	Class	Continue
def	del	elif	else	except
exec	finally	for	from	global
if	import	in	is	lambda
Not	or	pass	print	raise
return	try	while	with	yield

Indentation and Lines

There are no braces for the indication of blocks of code for class definition and function in Python. Likewise, flow control is not included. If you want to denote such blocks of code, you have to make use of line indentation. You can adjust it for spaces, but make sure to indent all statements with a block, too. To help you understand this further, consider the following sample codes:

```
if True:
print "Correct"
else:
print "Incorrect"
```

```
if True
print "Input"
print "Correct"
else:
```

```
print "Input"
print "False
```

Running the first given example generates an output. Running the second one, however, results in an error. Why did this happen? Well, you have to keep in mind that in Python, blocks are formed by indenting continuous lines with the same amount of space.

Indentation is simply a way to group statements. Programmers use it in place of curly braces of blocks of code. Tabs and spaces are supported, but standard indentation requires standard codes to have similar amounts of spaces. In general, four spaces are used. Take a look at the following example:

```
w = 1
if w == 1 :
```

```
    # This shows an indentation with exactly
four spaces
```

```
    print " w is 1 . "
```

Indentation Myths

There are certain myths that surround
indentation in Python. Here are some of
them:

A whitespace is necessary in every source code.

Actually, you do not have to use
whitespaces in all your source codes.
A whitespace is not necessarily
significant, although an indentation is.
As you have learned, this is the
whitespace found at the very left part
of a statement. Everywhere else, a
whitespace is not that significant and

may be omitted. You can use it in any way you like, even inserting arbitrary whitespaces or empty lines that do not contain anything anywhere in your program.

Moreover, the exact amount of indentation does not really matter, but the relative indentation of your nested blocks does. The indentation level is actually not recognized when you use implicit or explicit continuation lines. For instance, you may split a list across multiple lines. The indentation is just not significant at all. Take a look at the following example:

```
foo = [
' a string ' ,
' another string ' ,
' a short string '
```

```
]
print foo
```

If you run the above given code, you
will get the following output:

```
[ ' a string ' , ' another string ' , ' a
short string ' ]
```

Here is another example:

```
bar = ' look at this example ' \
' of a long string ' \
' that is split ' \
' across multiple lines '
print bar
```

If you run the above given code, you
will obtain the following output:

look at this example of a long string that is split across multiple lines

A certain style of indentation should be used in your programs.

Well, this one is both true and untrue. You can write the inner block on a line and not indent it. You can use any of the following versions of the "*if statement*" since all of them are valid and produce the same output:

```
if 1 + 1 == 2 :

    print " foo"

    print " bar "

    w = 99
```

```
if 1 + 1 == 2 :

        print "foo" ; print " bar " ; w
= 99


if 1 + 1 == 2 : print " foo " ; print "
bar " ; w = 99
```

As a programmer, you may wish to write your block of code in separate lines, such as the one shown in the first example. However, there are times when there are similar *if statements* that you can conveniently write on each line.

In case you decide to write your block of code on separate lines, then you have to follow the rules of indentation. You have to indent the enclosed block more than the *"if statement"*.

In conclusion, you will be forced to abide by this rule in Python, unless you opted to make the structure of your program more complicated. The programming language does not allow program structure obfuscation with the use of fake indentations.

Keep in mind that blocks are denoted by indentation in the Python programming language; thus, the indentation is the same in every program. The consistency of the code formatting makes the program easier to read and understand.

It is not possible to mix spaces and tabs in Python.

Yes, this one is true, even for programs written in the C language. You cannot mix spaces and tabs safely. Even though there would not really be a huge difference for your compiler, you may have a hard time dealing with codes. For instance, if you move a C source to one editor that has different tab stops, bugs will be easier to introduce.

Once again, keep in mind that it is not ideal to mix spaces and tabs for indentation. You can use spaces or tabs alone, though. In addition, you may want to avoid tabs altogether. After all, the semantics of tabs are not that well-defined and may appear differently on various types of editors and systems.

Tabs are also often wrongly converted or destroyed during copy and paste operations, as well as whenever a source code gets inserted into a Web page or any other type of markup code.

It is possible to skip the indentation and use a keyword instead.

Yes, you can skip using an indentation and just use a keyword. There are actually a few programmers who prefer to use *endif* instead of an indentation to indicate the end of a block of code.

Well, it is not exactly a recognized keyword in Python. The earlier versions of the programming language come with a tool that converts code using the keyword *end* to correct the indentation and remove such keyword.

This may be used as a pre-processor to the compiler. In the recent versions of the programming language, however, the tool has been removed, most probably because it is not often used.

How is the indentation parsed by the compiler?

The parsing is actually simple and well defined. In general, the changes to the level of indentation are inserted as tokens into the stream. The indentation levels are stored using a stack from the lexical analyzer or tokenizer. At first, the stack only has a value of 0, which is found at the leftmost part.

Each time a nested block starts, a new level of indentation gets pushed on the stack. The *indent token* is then inserted into the stream, which is eventually passed on to the parser. It is not possible to have more than a single indent token in succession.

In the event that a line is seen with a smaller level of indentation, the values start popping from the stack until one of them gets on top. This is equivalent to the new level of indentation. In case there is nothing found, a syntax error is generated. For ever value popped, there is a *dedent token*. It is possible to have multiple dedent tokens in succession. At the end of every source code, there are dedent tokens generated for the level of indentation that is left at the stack. This continues to occur until there is 0 left.

Multiline Statements

When you end a statement, you can either use a new line or a continuation symbol (\ ) if you want to indicate that the line needs to continue. To help you understand this concept further, consider the following example:

```
total = first_item + \
second_item + \
```

third_item

There is no need for you to use the continuation symbol when you write statements that are contained within brackets, such as { }, ( ), and [ ]. For instance, if you wish to display the months in a year, you may simply write:

year = ['January' , 'February' , 'March' , 'April' , 'May' , 'June' , 'July' , 'August' , 'September' , 'October' , 'November' , 'December']

You are allowed to write multiple statements on a single line or create multiple groups as suites. When it comes to writing multiple statements, keep in mind that the inclusion of the semicolon (;) is crucial. The semicolon allows you to write as many statements as possible, as long as they do not start a new block of code. Consider the following example:

```
import sys ; y = 'bar' ; sys.stdout.write ( y + '
\n ' )
```

So what are suites exactly? Well, they are groups of statements that consist of blocks of code. Compound or complex statements, such as *if*, *while*, *def*, and *class* require a suite and a header line.

So what are header lines? They begin statements with a keyword and end them with a colon (:) . Also, they are followed by one or more lines that make up a suite. Consider the following example:

```
if expression :
suite
elif expression :
suite
```

else :

suite

Quotation

As a programmer, you are allowed to use a single quote (') , double quote ("), and a triple quote ("' or """') when you denote string literals. Then again, see to it that you use the same type of quotes at the start and end of your string. Typically, triple quotes are used to span strings across multiple lines. Take a look at the following example:

paragraph = """" You are reading an example of a paragraph that consists multiple lines and sentences. You are an excellent programmer. """"

Comments

When it comes to comments, you should use the hash symbol (#) to start them. However, this hash symbol should not be within a string literal. Also, the characters after it towards the end of the line should be included in the comment. In Python, comments are not recognized by the interpreter. To help you understand this concept further, take a look at the following example:

```
# This is the first comment
print " Monty Python's Flying Circus is a British sketch comedy series. " ;
# This is the second comment
```

If you run the example given above, you will obtain the following output:
Monty Python's Flying Circus is a British sketch comedy series.

You can also write another comment after an expression or a statement, such as in the following:

name = "Wendy" # This is a sample comment

If you want to comment on multiple lines, you may do so as well. For example:

This is a sample comment.
This one is also a comment.
This is another comment.
This comment is written by Wendy.

Blank Lines

These lines are not recognized in the Python programming language. With this being said, they are pretty much like comments. They contain whitespaces and even comments. You have to use empty lines to terminate multiline statements in an interactive interpreter session.

Chapter 3: Data Types

In Python, input data are sorted according to different categories. The primary purpose of sorting is to help programmers like you in processing information more efficiently. Such categories function as data storage locations that you can access whenever you run the Python platform.

Variables

Variables contain values that have been specifically allocated to them. If you are working on complex codes for applications, you may want to store your information in these variables. Do not worry because you can access them anytime you need them. You can even use them to ensure that the information you gather from your end users stay safe and secured.

Numeric Types

Numbers in the Python programming language are different from the numbers you use to solve problems in Algebra. In Mathematics, adding *.0* at the end of a number practically means nothing. It does not make any difference to its value. For instance, *3* and *3.0* are the same.

In Python, however, *3* and *3.0* are different numbers. Before the program processes it, it has to undergo certain data processing methods. As a programmer, you have to learn about the different numeric types.

Integers

All whole numbers are integers. Numbers that contain a decimal point are not whole numbers; therefore, 3 is a whole number while 3.0 is not. Integers in Python are characterized by the data type *int*.

Take note that integers have capacity limitations. You will generate an error if you try to process a value beyond the allowed limits. Integers typically process numbers between -9,223,372,036.854 and 9,223,372,036.854.

There are interesting features that come with the *int* variable. For instance, base 2 only uses 0 and 1, base 8 uses numbers from 0 to 7, base 10 has similar properties with the decimal system and base 16 uses the letters A to F and the numbers 0 to 9 as digits.

Floating Point Values

Any number that contains a decimal point is considered as a floating point value in Python. It does not matter if the number after the decimal point is *0* or not. *3.0*, *1.5*, and *11.4*, for example, are all floating point values. They are stored in the float data type. One huge advantage of floating point values over integers is that they have bigger storage spaces; hence, they are capable of storing very small or large values.

Then again, you should not think that they have an unlimited storage space. There is still a limitation. Nevertheless, they can contain as little as $\pm 2.2250738585072014 \times 10^{-308}$ and as much as $1.7976931348623157 \times 10^{-308}$. There are a couple of ways to allocate values with the use of floating point values. First, you can directly assign them. Second, you can use a scientific notation. Keep in mind that negative exponents produce fraction equivalents.

Complex Numbers

These numbers consist of real numbers and imaginary numbers combined. Usually, they are used in dynamic systems, quantum mechanics, computer graphics, electrical engineering and fluid dynamics. Complex numbers can be processed in Python and a few other programming languages.

Boolean Values

These are the two constant objects *True* and *False*. They represent truth values. When used in a numeric context, they function as 0 and 1. You can use the function *bool* to assign a value to a Boolean if such value may be interpreted as a truth value.

Strings

They are groups of characters that are connected with double quotation marks. Consider the following example:

TheString = " Python got its name from a popular comedy show. "

As you can see in the sample code shown above, the phrase *Python got its name from a popular comedy show.* is assigned to the variable *TheString.*

Computers cannot understand letters, only numbers. So when you write a program, Python reads and interprets it based on the numbers that represent its letters. For example, in the American Standard Code for Information Interchange (ASCII), the number *65* represents the letter *A*. So if you type in

ord (" A ")

you will get an output of 65

Because computers cannot understand letters, you have to convert strings into numbers. You can use *int* or *float* to do this. In case you need to convert numbers into strings, you can use *str*.

Chapter 4: Operators

The values of your operands are manipulated by operators. There are seven types of operators used in the Python programming language. The following tables display these operators and provide brief explanations regarding their function.

Arithmetic Operators

Operator	Description
Addition (+)	It adds the values.
Subtraction (-)	It subtracts the second operand from the previous operand.
Multiplication	It multiples the values.

(*)	
Division (/)	It divides the first operand by the second operand.
Modulus (%)	It divides the first operand by the second operand and returns the remainder
Exponent (**)	It performs exponential calculation on the operators.
Floor Division (//)	It divides the operands but eliminates the decimal points after the result.

Comparison Operators or Relational Operators

Operator	Description
==	If the values of both operands are equal, the condition is true.
!=	If the values of both operands are not equal, the condition is true.
<>	If the values of both operands are not equal, the condition is true.
>	If the value of the left operand is bigger than the value of the right operand, the condition is true.
<	If the value of the left operand is less than the value of the right operand, the condition is true.

>=	If the value of the left operand is bigger or equal to the value of the right operand, the condition is true.
<=	If the value of the left operand is less than or equal to the value of the right operand, the condition is true.

Assignment Operators

Operator	*Description*
=	It assigns values from the right operand to the left operand.
+= add AND	It adds the right operand to the left operand, and then allocates the result to the left

	operand.
-= subtract AND	It subtracts the right operand from the left operand, and then allocates the result to the left operand.
*= multiply AND	It multiples the left operand and the right operand, and then allocates the result to the left operand.
/= divide AND	It divides the left operand with the right operand, and then allocates the result to the left operand.
%= modulus AND	It uses the two operands to find the modulus, and then allocates the result to the left

	operand.
**= exponent AND	It performs exponential computation on the operators and then assigns the value to the left operand.
//= floor division	It performs floor division on the operators and assigns the value to the left operand.

Bitwise Operators

Operator	Description
& binary AND	It copies the bit if it is present in both operands.
| binary OR	It copies the bit if it is present in either operand.
^ binary XOR	It copies the bit if it is present in one operand, but not both.
~ binary ones complement	It flips bits.
<< binary left shift	It moves the value of the left operand towards the left based on the number of bits assigned by the right

	operand.
`>>` binary right shift	It moves the value of the left operand towards the right based on the number of bits assigned by the right operand.

Logical Operators

Operator	Description
And logical AND	The condition is true if both operands are true.
Or logical OR	The condition is true if an operand is non-zero.
Not logical	It reverses the logical state of

NOT	the operand.

Membership Operators

Operator	Description
Is	If the variables on either side of the operator point toward the same object, it evaluates to true. Otherwise, it evaluates to false.
Not in	If it does not find a variable in a particular sequence, it evaluates to true. Otherwise, it evaluates to false.

Identity Operators

Operator	Description
Is	If the variables on either side of the operator point towards the same object, it evaluates to true. Otherwise, it evaluates to false.
Is not	If the variables on either side of the operator point towards the same object, it evaluates to false. Otherwise, it evaluates to true.

Conclusion

Thank you again for downloading this book!

I hope this book was able to help you learn about the Python programming language.

The next step is to apply what you have learned from this book. Finally, if you enjoyed this book, then I'd like to ask you for a favor, would you be kind enough to leave a review for this book on Amazon? It'd be greatly appreciated!

Please leave a review on Amazon!

Thank you and good luck!

Windows 10 Academy

The Stress Free Way To Learning
Windows 10 Inside & Out

Table Of Contents

Introduction

I want to thank you and congratulate you for downloading the book, *"Windows 10: Beginner's User Guide to Mastering Windows 10"*.

Haven't got Windows 10 yet? Well, where have you been and what have you been doing?

Sure, it may be nice to stay comfortable with Windows 7 or 8, but it would be so much better to switch to Windows 10—along with the rest of the world!

While it may seem confusing at first, navigating Windows 10 isn't actually that hard to learn. All you need is the right guide—and with the help of this book, you'll be able to master Windows 10 in no time.

Read this book now to find out how.

Thanks again for downloading this book, I hope you enjoy it!

Chapter 1: What's New?

One of the very first things you'll notice about Windows 10 is that while the Charms Bar is still there, you can use Windows 10 without it.

Ever since Windows 8 was created, the Charms Bar has already been there. The problem with it, though, is that a lot of people feel like it's not really helpful and it just makes the interface confusing.

In Windows 10, you can just hide the Charms Bar—but make sure to hide the System Tray Icon first. Here's how:

Hide Tray Temporarily

There are two ways to hide the system tray. First is the temporary fix which goes like this:

1. If you cannot see all the items that you need in the tray, just click right under the arrow.

2. Now, if all the icons are present, go ahead and open the task manager (CTRL+ALT+DEL), then terminate GWUX/GWXUX Process.

Hide Tray Permanently

Now, if you really feel like you're not ever going to use the tray, you can hide it permanently by doing the following:

1. Go to *Control Panel > Windows Update*.

2. Choose *Installed Updates* on the left side of the screen, followed by *View Installed Updates*. You'll now seeInstalled Updates on top of the screen.

3. When you see the update labeled *Update for Microsoft Windows KB3035583*, go ahead and remove it.

4. Just skip this update if it shows up another time, just in case.

Hide the Charms Bar

Then, you can proceed to hide the Charms Bar.

Basically, you can just choose *Settings* on its own, instead of having it appear in the Charms Menu. By clicking *Settings*, you're already able to turn off the Charms Bar.

In order to access full Settings without the Charms Bar, here's what you have to do:

1. Click *Charms* Bar.

2. Click *Change PC Settings*.

3. Then, access the first screen that you'd see on Windows 10.

4. Click the Start Button so that the new Start Menu would be displayed.

5. Click the *Settings* link.

6. Voila! You're all set!

Chapter 2: The Emergence of Cortana

Another newest incarnation in Windows 10 is *Cortana,* a virtual assistant who will be able to help you search for what you need in your computer, find files, track packages, manage your calendar, and even chat with you—especially when you need help with something!

You can access Cortana simply by typing a question on the search bar that you'll see on top of the taskbar. You can also use the microphone icon to do this—however, it's best to just search because not all phones (in case you've synced Windows 10 with your other devices, too) have clear microphones/speakers.

The Magic Word

You can let Cortana respond to you every time you say the words *Hey, Cortana.* To do this, just:

1. Select Notebook > Settings.

2. You'll see a setting that says *Let Cortana respond when you say Hey, Cortana.* Turn that option on.

What It Does

Cortana will be able to help you out with a lot of things, but mostly here's what you can expect:

1. Ask Cortana about weather conditions. Learning what the weather will be like is extremely helpful because it allows you to plan your events accordingly.

Simply ask *what is the weather in (location of choice),* and Cortana will be able to answer you. You can also click Cortana's *Noteboo*k, click *Weathe*r, and see what the day has in store for you!

2. Get Reminders based on locations. This means you'd ask Cortana to remind you of something while you're at a particular location. For example, when you're at the grocery and want to be reminded that you need to buy *cat food, you can tell Cortana: Remind* me to buy cat food while at Park Avenue Grocery— or something to that effect. Just make sure you don't forget to say *Remind Me* because that's the magic phrase here. You can also tell Cortana to edit or turn off the

reminders that you already have made in order to avoid confusion.

3. Let Cortana open apps for you! Finally, you can let Cortana open the apps you need by saying *Open (desired app)*. For example, *Cortana, open Adobe Photoshop*. See, now you'd be able to do what you have to do—even without making use of your hands!

4. Let Cortana search for media files according to time. Searching could be daunting if you have no idea where to start, and if there are just too much information on one page. What you can do then is let Cortana search by file type, or by date. For example, say *Cortana, search for music from 3 years ago*. Make sure you have the files you need

on your PC or on OneDrive—or you could also connect Cortana with Edge (learn more on Chapter 7) to do this.

5. Let Cortana sing for you! Yes, Cortana isn't just informative, she's entertaining, too. What you can do is allow her to sing for you, and even sings with Jen Taylor's human voice! This way, you wouldn't be scared or think that she's so robotic. To make her sing, you can use the following commands:

6. Let her know your preferences by telling her about myself. Simply type or say *let me tell you about myself*, and begin to tell her about your likes and dislikes, and what makes

you happy, or what it is that you want to learn more about.

Sing me a lullaby.

Sing me a song.

What does the fox say?

Set those Reminders

Cortana could also help you set reminders for important things that are going on. You can do this simply by going to the search bar and typing whatever you want to be reminded of. For example:

1. Wake me up at 6 on Saturday for the meeting.

2. Remind me of the Superbowl.

3. Change my 9am to 10:30.

Easter Eggs

Using Cortana becomes even more fun with the help of Easter Eggs! These are things you could ask or tell Cortana which would give really humorous and interesting answers!

Here are the best ones you should try:

1. Do you like Google Now?

2. Can you dance?

3. Who's better: You or Siri?

4. Are you awake?

5. I hate you.

Switching Cortana Off

If you're tired of Cortana or don't need her help anymore, you can simply turn the function off by going to *Settings*, and then choosing *turn Cortana off*.

Chapter 3: Using the Start Menu

A lot of users say that the Windows 10 Start Menu is quite confusing, but it's not impossible to understand it. Here are simple steps that you could follow in order for you to use it!

1. Click the *Start* Menu. This will appear on the left side of the screen.

2. Click *All Apps*. Again, this'll be on the left side of the screen. You'll then see a display of all the apps installed on your computer.

3. The *Power* button would then allow you to rest or shut Windows down. This is found on the left column of the screen.

4. To lock the PC, just right-click your account name and then you'd see the following options: *lock, change account picture, sign out*. Choose lock.

5. To manage the tiles you see on the right side of the screen, just right-click on a tile, and then you'd see a menu pop up onscreen. Choose either *Unpin from Start, Resize* or *Pin to Taskbar*. Also check if there is an *Uninstall* option—this would come with most apps.

6. To search for an app or file, type what you're looking for in the *Search Field* and you'll see a list of choices popping up onscreen.

7. You can also pin certain items on the Start Menu. To do this, just

right click on the file you'd like to see on the Start Menu and then *click Pin to Start.*

Accessing the Secret Menu

There is such a thing as the "Secret Start Menu"—but now, it's not *that* secret anymore, isn't it? Here's how you can access it.

1. Right click on the *Start* icon.

2. You will then see a pop-up menu with mostly everything you can do with the computer!

3. If using touchscreen, you can access this menu by tapping and holding he start button for at least 5 to 10 seconds!

Customizing the Start menu

Of course, you could also personalize or customize the menu based on your own preferences!

1. To make a switch between the Start Menu and the Start Screen, open *Settings > Personalization > Start > Start Behaviors > Use Fullscreen Start when in Desktop.*

2. To customize what you'll see onscreen, go to Settings > Customize. There, you'll see a list of suggested apps from Microsoft. Another setting would show you setting controls for your recently opened programs, and the last one would be about *Jump List* items.

3. To change the color of the Start Menu, window borders, and

taskbar, go to *Settings* > *Personalization* > *Colors.* If you want a brightly colored PC, just go to *Show Color on Start, Taskbar, and Action Center,* and it'll happen.

4. Click *Start* to see whether you have all the folders and files that you need.

5. Click *Start* > *Choose Folders* to choose which folders you'd like to see onscreen.

Using Start Menu and Start Screen at the Same Time

If you need to do a lot of things at once and if you hate waiting, maybe it's good for you to start using both the Start Menu and Start Screen at the same time! Here's how:

1. Click *Start* button, followed by *Settings > Personalization.*

2. Click *Start.*

3. Choose *Use Start FullScreen.*

4. Click Start Screen to make Start Menu disappear.

5. Uncheck *Use Start FullScreen* to return to *Settings.*

6. Then, you can also resize the Start Menu. To do this, click *Start.*

7. Move cursor to the top of the Start Menu, and then drag and move it up to the top of the said Menu. To decrease the height, just drag the cursor down.

8. Increase width by dragging cursor to the right, and drag it to the left to decrease.

Changing the Log-In Screen

Another thing you can do is change the log-in
screen to make it suited to your preferences.
Some people find the log-in screen to be too
shiny and tacky, and if you're one of those
people, you can make things easier by doing
the following:

> 1. Go to *Settings* > *Personalization* >
>   *Lock Screen.*
>
> 2. Scroll down and once the screen
>   toggles, you'll see *Show Windows
>   Background Picture on Sign-In Screen.*
>
> 3. Turn the said toggle off so that
>   the next time you'd log-in, you'd
>   only see the Windows logo on the
>   screen.

You can also tweak this in the registry by
doing the following:

1. Go to *Start > All Apps > Windows System > Run.*

2. In the dialog box, type *regedit,* and then press Enter.

3. Navigate   to *HKEY_LOCAL_MACHINE> Software>Policies>Microsoft Windows>System* in the Registry Editor.

4. Now, right click System and then click *New>DWORD(32 bit) Value.*

5. Change the label to *DWORD Disable Log-in Background Image* (without spaces)

6. Right click *Disable Log-in Background Image* and choose *Modify.*

7. Type *1* under *Value Data* and Click OK.

8. Press *Windows Key* + *L* together so that you'll see a flat color background once you log in.

9. Go to *Settings* > *Personalization* > *Background* to tweak the color of the background, if desired.

Chapter 4: Managing Settings

One of the biggest differences of Windows 10 from its predecessors is the fact that upon turning the computer on, you'll see not just a Start Menu, but also a Settings Menu. This one opens in a new window, with big, touch-friendly icons. Unlike menus that are hiding from the Charms Menu in Windows 7 and 8, this one appears right away—which makes it more comfortable for you.

Some of the things you could find in this menu include:

Managing Devices

The Settings Menu introduces a couple of devices that you can use while using this Operating System. This also talks about the devices you can connect with your PC while on this Operating System. Here's what you can do:

1. First up is *Autoplay* allows you to choose whether Autoplay should be switched on or off.

2. *Typing* allows you to choose whether you'd like to use a physical or onscreen keyboard.

3. *Printers and Scanners* allows you to add printers to your computer. To do this, just click *Devices and Printers> Device Manager> Related Settings> Add a Printer or Scanner* and follow the instructions you'll see onscreen.

4. *Mouse and Touchpad* gives you a chance to configure Mouse and Touchpad settings. Just choose

Mouse and Touchpad > Related Settings> Additional Mouse Options.

5. *Connected Devices*, meanwhile, is about other connected devices that are not printers or scanners.

Taking Care of Accounts

Aside from your own account, you could also manage the account of your family members—as long as they are connected to your own!

Here's what you need to know:

1. *Your Account* is your primary sign-in account. This is linked to Microsoft's Cloud Network.

2. *Work Access* tells you whether the
   PC or your account is connected
   to another network.

3. *Sync Your Settings* allows you to
   sync this PC with your other
   gadgets—and other computers at
   home, as well. This way, it would
   be easy for you to control them
   even if you are away from home.

4. *Sign-in options* will ask you how
   exactly you want to open your
   computer. You can make use of
   normal log-in plus password,
   choose Windows Hello, which
   would allow you to log in using
   biometrics.

5. *Family and Other Users* allows you
   to add more admins to the PC. To
   do this, just click *Set up account for*

assigned access > Choose an Account >
Choose an App.

Customizing and Personalization

To customize and personalize your settings,
just do the following:

1. *Background* is mainly just the
   wallpaper of your computer, and
   choose how you'd want the photo
   to fit on your screen.

2. *Colors* are the colors that would be
   used for your desktop, toolbars,
   etc.

3. *Lockscreen* is what you'll see
   onscreen while it is locked. Click
   Pictures, and you'll see the 5 recent
   lockscreen pictures used, as well as
   a *Browse* button for you to choose

photos from your files. Choosing *Slideshow* would make a slideshow of pictures as your lockscreen. You can also choose *Screen Timeout*, and more *Screen Saver Settings*, as well.

4. Themes would help you choose which theme you'd like to use. Go to *Classic Theme Settings* > *Related Settings* to do this.

5. Start helps you turn applications and notifications on or off—and more. You'd learn more about this in the next chapter.

Updating and Restoration

In case something goes wrong or you receive notifications regarding updates, here's what you have to do:

1. *Activation* is about the version of Windows that you have, and gives you the chance to change Product Key.

2. *Advanced Options* would give you more Update settings to choose from.

3. *Backup* gives you the chance to backup your settings.

4. Click *Check for Updates* so you could check for updates manually.

5. *For Developers* is all about making apps and programs while on Windows 10.

6. *Recovery* contains options that you can use to fix your computer, which are: *Reset PC, Go back to Earlier Build*, and *Advanced Startup*.

7. The tab named *Windows Update* contains everything you'd ever need to update Windows.

8. *Windows Defender*, meanwhile, is your cloud protection system.

9.

Networks and Internet

Who can live without the internet these days? You can tweak your internet and network settings in Windows 10 in a fast and easy manner—you can do it this way.

1. *Data Usage* is mostly about the bandwidth that is being used, and is mostly about connected devices that work on Wi-Fi.

2. *VPN* is about adding a VPN Connection to your PC. To tweak this, just go to *PC Settings* >

Network > *Add VPN Connection* > *Related Settings* > *Show Available Connections.*

3. *Dial-up and Ethernet* are your old-school Internet settings that work on IVP 4.

4. *Proxy* will allow you to decide whether you'd use a manual or automatic Proxy. You can check this out by going to *PC Settings* > *Network* > *Proxy.*

Turning Off Wi-Fi Sharing

In order to make sure that your Wi-Fi connection stays yours, and that you would have more privacy, you can disable Wi-Fi sharing! Here's how:

Go to *Settings > Network and Internet > Wi-Fi > Manage Wi-Fi Settings.* You can also turn off networks that automatically connect to Skype, Quora, Outlook or Facebook, as well.

Making Accounts Private

These days, it's so important to keep your accounts private. It would be a good way of protecting yourself and the people you care for from people who might phish information from you. Windows 10 makes this easy. For this, you can try:

> 1. *Account Info, Calendar, Contacts, Messaging, Radio* just gives you permission whether you'd like to sync them with other devices or not.

2. *Location* basically works on GPS, and allows you whether you'd like to let others see where you are or not.

3. *General* is about deciding whether you'd like your name to appear on apps, programs, photos, and any other file that is connected to your computer.

4. *Feedback.* Choose whether you'd want Microsoft to ask you for feedback *once a day, once a week, automatically, always,* or *never.*

5. *Speech, Inking, Typing* mostly gives you the option to use Cortana (Windows 10's digital assistant) or not.

6. *Other Devices* gives you permission to sync Xbox One and

information found there with your Microsoft account.

7. *Microphone* gives you the chance to turn the microphone on or off.

Chapter 5: Playing with Features

Upgrading to Windows 10 means you'd be able to experience a bevy of fascinating features that you could use in your day to day life! This way, you'd get to enjoy Windows 10 even more!

Import Bookmarks First

If you have been using other browsers before and want to regain access to bookmarks you've made there, you can just import them to the Edge. Here's how:

1. Open Edge and click "…", then click Settings.

2. Choose Import Favorites from Another Browser.

3. Choose all the browsers you want to import bookmarks from and you're all set!

Using the Photos App

1. Take note that the Photos App now has two main features, and these are: *Collections* and *Albums.* Your photos are chronologically arranged by date in the *Collections* tab. Meanwhile, *Albums* contain albums that the app has created automatically for you.

2. To add a folder, go to *Settings > Sources > Add a Folder > Add this Folder to Pictures.*

3. To show photos and videos from *OneDrive,* just choose Settings >

Show my Photos and Videos from OneDrive.

4. To share pictures, just select the picture you want to share and click *Share*!

5. You can also make use of Filters and other Editing Features, as well!

Picking Default Programs

You can change default programs and protocols by following the instructions below:

1. Open *Settings* > *System* > *Default Apps*.

2. Change the programs you'd want to use for email, calendar, maps, web browser, video player, photo viewer, and the like.

3. To set individual file types, go to *Settings > System > Choose Default Apps by File Type.*

4. To set defaults for protocols, go to *Settings > System > Choose Default Apps by Protocol.*

5. To change default programs, just go to *Settings > System > Set Defaults by App > Set Default Programs > Set Program as Default > Choose Defaults for this Program*

Sideloading Apps

Sideloading is important because it allows you to install apps that are not available in the Windows Store. Here's how you can do it:

1. Open *Settings > Update and Security.*

2. Go to *For Developers* > *Sideload Apps*.

3. You will now receive a warning about sideloading being dangerous. Just click *Yes* to say that you understand the risks.

Managing Pop-Ups

You can also delay shutter speed in capturing screenshots by making sure that you get to capture pop-ups, too. Here's how:

1. Open *Snipping Tool* and then click *Delay*. Choose between numbers 0 to 5.

2. Choose the type of *Snip* that you'd like to make by clicking what you find next to *New*. Choose from

window, rectangular, free-form, full-screen.

3. Click *New* so you could begin snipping. You will now have an allowance of 0 to 5 seconds, depending on what you chose earlier. The screen will freeze and you'll be able to capture the image you want.

4. Click *Save* to save your screenshot.

5.

Fast File Sharing

1. Look for the file that you'd want to share.

2. Click *Sharing* in the *File Explorer.*

3. Click *Share* button.

4. Choose the program you'd want to share the said file with.

5. Configure options by going to *Settings > System > Share Lab*.

Chapter 6: Making Use of Microsoft Edge

Microsoft Edge is Windows 10's main web browser. It's quite a customizable, easy to enjoy browser. Here are just some of the things that you could do with it!

Microsoft Edge Reading View is also a great innovation because it clears out all distractions that could prevent you from doing what you want online, especially if it's work-related! To make use of this, you could just click *Book* on the top left corner of Edge to activate Reading View!

Edge Customization

1. Click *Menu > Settings > Open With*.

2. Now, you can choose how your Start and tab pages will look like!

3. You can also customize tab pages. What you have to do is click Settings > Open New Tabs With, and then choose the option that you want from what would appear onscreen!

Webpage Annotation

The great thing about Edge is that it allows you to highlight, write, or draw on a webpage. This way, you can easily save and share it, edited the way you want! To do this, simply click the *Pen and Paper* icon on top of the page!

Playing with Webpages

You can also delay shutter speed in capturing screenshots by making sure that you get to capture pop-ups, too. Here's how:

1. Open *Snipping Tool* and then click *Delay*. Choose between numbers 0 to 5.

2. Choose the type of *Snip* that you'd like to make by clicking what you find next to *New*. Choose from window, rectangular, free-form, full-screen.

3. Click *New* so you could begin snipping. You will now have an allowance of 0 to 5 seconds, depending on what you chose earlier. The screen will freeze and you'll be able to capture the image you want.

4. Click *Save* to save your screenshot.

Creating Article List

You could also create a list of articles that you want to read while in Reading View. To do so, just:

1. Click the *Star Icon* when you find an article that you like.

2. Navigate to *Reading List*, and then click *Add*.

You can also pin webpages/websites to the Start Menu. Just click *Pin to Start* while browsing a webpage and you'll be able to pin the website on the Start Menu.

Private Browsing

You can also browse privately while using Edge. This way, whatever it is that you searched for/visited would not appear in the

Browser History. To do so, just click *Browse in Private Window* and you're all set!

Caret Browsing

This literally means that you'll be able to browse webpages with the use of your keyboard—even without using the mouse!

To do this, simply press *F7* and then confirm the prompt you see onscreen!

Integration with Cortana

You can also use Cortana while on Edge! Simply Pin Cortana to Edge, and you'll be able to make use of the said feature more!

Integration with Flash

With the help of flash integration, you'd be able to watch HD videos on Edge. You can also turn this feature on or off. To help you with this, you should:

1. Go to *Settings* > *Advanced Settings* > *Use Adobe Flash Player*.

2. Choose whether you'd like to turn it on or off.

Chapter 7: Maximizing the Use of Windows 10

And of course, in order to appreciate Windows 10 more, you should try to maximize the use of it with the help of the instructions mentioned in this chapter!

Real Time Notifications

Since Windows 10 proves to be the Operating System for the new age, you can expect it to give you real time notifications. In short, you'll get notifications from *Facebook, Twitter, Instagram,* and any other apps you might be using—as long as they're connected to your Microsoft account.

> 1. To choose which notifications you'd like to have, go to *Action Center > Show Notifications from*

These Apps. There, you'd see a list of the apps you have. Just choose what notifications you'd like to have and you're all set!

2. You can also choose which Quick Actions you'd like to have access to. To do this, go to *Settings > System > Notifications and Actions > Choose Your Quick Actions.*

Open Programs Quickly

1. Go to *Start Menu > All Apps.*

2. Look for the app you'd want to make a shortcut for and then right click on it. You will then see a dropdown menu. Choose *Open File Location,* and then skip the next step that will pop up onscreen.

3. Once you've found the app, click and drag it from the *Start Menu* all the way to the desktop. Right-click and then choose *Properties*.

4. Now, the *Properties* window will open up onscreen. Look for the Shortcut tab and then choose Shortcut Key. Tap the key you'd want to be associated with the app (i.e., CTRL + ALT + [chosen key]).

5. Click *Continue*.

6. You can now use your chosen shortcut to open this certain app!

The Quick Access Feature

A lot of people say that *Quick Access* makes Windows 10 a whole lot more manageable—and there is a lot of truth to that. You can learn more about it below:

1. To add a file to *Quick Access*, just navigate towards the file you want to add, and then simply click Add to Quick Access.

2. To remove a file from *Quick Access*, go to the said file and click Unpin from Quick Access.

3. To remove recently used files and frequently used folders from *Quick Access,* just go to *View > Options > General > Privacy.* Then, uncheck the boxes that say *Show Recently Used Files.* Click *Clear > Clear File*

Explorer History. You can also choose Hide or Hide from Recent.

4. To change the way File Explorer opens, just *click View > Options > Open File Explorer > This PC.*

The Snap Assist

This is a feature that is exclusive for Windows 10! This helps you snap a certain window to a certain side of the screen so you won't spend lots of time moving it around.

> 1. To snap a window with the mouse, click on its title and drag it towards the side of the screen. You will then see an outline that will show you where the window would appear once you have dragged it.

2. To snap with the keyboard, just press Windows Key + Left Arrow (or Right Arrow).

3. To snap to one of the quadrants, just press Windows Key + Up Arrow (or Down Arrow), and then move it around by pressing Windows Key and arrow keys together.

Using Multiple Desktops at Once

Yes, you can make use of multiple "desktops" while using Windows 10. To make this happen, just follow the instructions below:

1. Add a desktop by clicking Task View. Press Tab + Windows Key > New Desktop.

2. Now, you have two virtual desktops. To switch between them, just press Windows Key + CTRL + Left Arrow + Windows Key + CTRL + Right Arrow.

3. To move windows between desktops, just right click on the window you'd want to move, then choose where you'd want to move it to.

To close the desktop, just click X or press Windows Key + CTRL + F4.

Shortcuts for the Command Prompt

You can also make use of keyboard shortcuts for the Command Prompt. Here's how:

Go to Start Menu > All Apps > Windows System > Command Prompt.

Click Properties > Options > Edit Options > Enable CTRL Key Shortcuts.

Now, here's a list of shortcuts you could use:

Shift + Up/Down (Move cursor up or down one line and then select text)

CTRL + V or Shift + Insert (paste copied text)

CTRL + C or CTRL + Insert (copy selected text to clipboard)

CTRL + A (select all in the current line)

CTRL + Page Up/Down (move screen one page up or down)

CTRL + Up/Down (move one line up or down)

CTRL + M (enter mark mode)

CTRL + F (open Find Window from the Command Prompt)

Alt + F4 (close command prompt)

CTRL + Shift + Home/End (move cursor to the beginning/end of screen buffer, and then select text and beginning/end of output)

Shift + Home/End (move cursor to beginning/end of current line and select text)

Shift + Page Up/Down (move cursor up/down screen and select text)

CTRL + Shift + Left/Right (move cursor left/right and select text)

Shift + Left/Right (move cursor left/right one character and select text)

Up/Down/Left/Right (In mark mode; move cursor up, down, left, or right)

Other Shortcuts

Here are more keyboard shortcuts that will certainly be helpful for you!

1. *Windows Key + Left* (Snap Window to Left Side of Screen)

2. *Windows Key + Right* (Snap Window to Right Side of Screen)

3. *Windows Key + Up/Down* (Snap Window to Quadrant)

4. *Windows Key + Tab* (Task View)

5. *Windows Key + CTRL + Left* (Go back to previous virtual desktop)

6. *Windows Key + CTRL + Right* (Go to next virtual desktop)

7. *Windows Key + CTRL + F4* (Close current virtual desktop)

8. *Windows Key + CTRL + D* (Create new virtual desktop)

Conclusion

Thank you again for downloading this book!

I hope this book was able to help you to understand windows 10 and learn how to use it without having a hard time!

The next step is to make sure that you follow the steps mentioned here and consult this book whenever you feel confused about using Windows 10.

Finally, if you enjoyed this book, then I'd like to ask you for a favor, would you be kind enough to leave a review for this book on Amazon? It'd be greatly appreciated!

Please leave a review on Amazon!

Thank you and good luck!

www.ingramcontent.com/pod-product-compliance
Lightning Source LLC
Chambersburg PA
CBHW071219050326
40689CB00011B/2378